D1736704

SLOTHS

MARYSA STORM

BLACK
RABBIT
BOOKS

Bolt Jr. is published by Black Rabbit Books
P.O. Box 3263, Mankato, Minnesota, 56002.
www.blackrabbitbooks.com
Copyright © 2020 Black Rabbit Books

Catherine Cates, designer; Omay Ayres, photo researcher

Names: Storm, Marysa, author.
Title: Sloths / by Marysa Storm.
Description: Mankato, Minnesota : Black Rabbit Books,
[2020] | Series: Bolt Jr. Awesome animal lives |
Audience: Age 6-8. | Audience: K to Grade 3. | Includes
bibliographical references and index.
Identifiers: LCCN 2018055720 (print) | LCCN 2018056491
(ebook) | ISBN 9781623101619 (e-book) |
ISBN 9781623101558 (library binding) |
ISBN 9781644661055 (paperback)
Subjects: LCSH: Sloths–Juvenile literature.
Classification: LCC QL737.E2 (ebook) | LCC QL737.E2 S76
2020 (print) | DDC 599.3/13–dc23
LC record available at https://lccn.loc.gov/2018055720

Printed in the United States. 5/19

Image Credits
Alamy: Avalon/Photoshot License, 10–11; FLPA, 16–17;
peruvianppictures.com: 8–9; National Geographic Creative: Roy
Toft, 5; National Geographic Photo Archive: Joel Sartore, 4; iStock:
Freder, 22–23; Shutterstock: alexavol, 7; Crazy nook, 3, 24;
Cuson, 12–13; Damsea, Cover, 13; Kertu, 6–7; Kristel Segeren, 1;
Nacho Such, 10; Rene Holtslag, 21; yod67, 14; Superstock: James
Christensen / Minden Pictures, 20–21; Suzi Eszterhas / Minden
Pictures, 19

Contents

CHAPTER 1

A Day in the Life

A hairy sloth hangs from a branch. Slowly, it grabs a leaf. The sloth **munches** it. Then it grabs another. The sloth chews it too. The animal looks like it's moving in slow motion. It isn't in a hurry.

munch: to eat or chew

WEIGHT COMPARISON

female
two-toed sloth
about 13 pounds
(6 kilograms)

Slow Movers

Sloths are slow animals. But they aren't lazy. They climb trees and eat. They also use their claws to protect themselves. Several animals eat them.

American shorthair cat
up to 15 pounds
(7 kg)

hair

claws

PARTS OF A Sloth

eyes

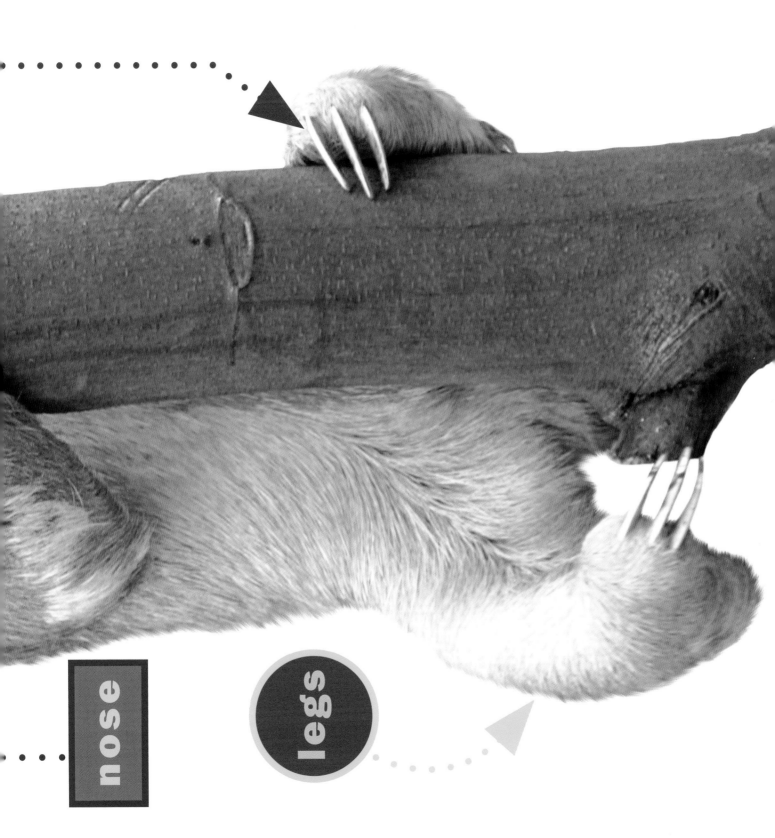

nose

legs

CHAPTER 2

Food and Homes

Sloths have a small **diet**. They mostly eat leaves. They also eat twigs and fruit. Their food doesn't give them much **energy**. They save energy by moving slowly.

diet: the food or drink usually taken in

energy: ability to be active

FACT

Sloths are most active at night.

Sloth Homes

Sloths live in Central and South America. They make their homes in **rain forests**. They spend most of their time in trees. They hang upside down from the branches. They sleep upside down too.

rain forest: a tropical forest that gets a lot of rain and has tall trees

Where Sloths Live

KEY

 = where sloths live

CHAPTER 3

Family Life

Sloths are not very social. They don't live in groups or even pairs. Instead, they live alone. Only mothers and babies live together.

FACT
Big wild cats eat sloths. So do snakes.

Babies

Babies hang from trees with their mothers. They live together for about a year. The mothers feed the babies. They show the babies what to eat too. Then the babies go off on their own.

.75

Newborn Two-Toed Sloth's Weight

about .75 pound
(.3 kg)

Bonus Facts

They have
18 teeth.

Sloths sleep
about 16
hours
each day.

They poop once a week.

They are excellent swimmers.

excellent: very good

21

READ MORE/WEBSITES

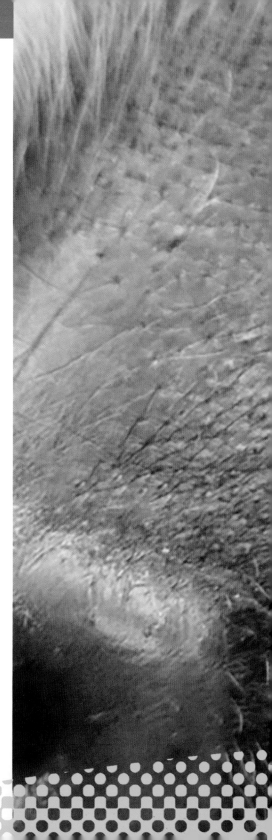

Beer, Julie. *Sharks vs. Sloths.* Washington, DC: National Geographic Kids, 2019.

Bozzo, Linda. *How Sloths Grow Up.* Animals Growing Up. New York: Enslow Publishing, 2020.

Wild, Margaret. *The Sloth Who Slowed Us Down.* New York: Abrams Books for Young Readers, 2018.

Fun Sloth Facts for Kids
www.sciencekids.co.nz/sciencefacts/animals/sloth.html

Meet Our Sloth!
kids.sandiegozoo.org/videos/meet-our-sloth

Sloth
kids.nationalgeographic.com/animals/sloth/#sloth-beach-upside-down.jpg

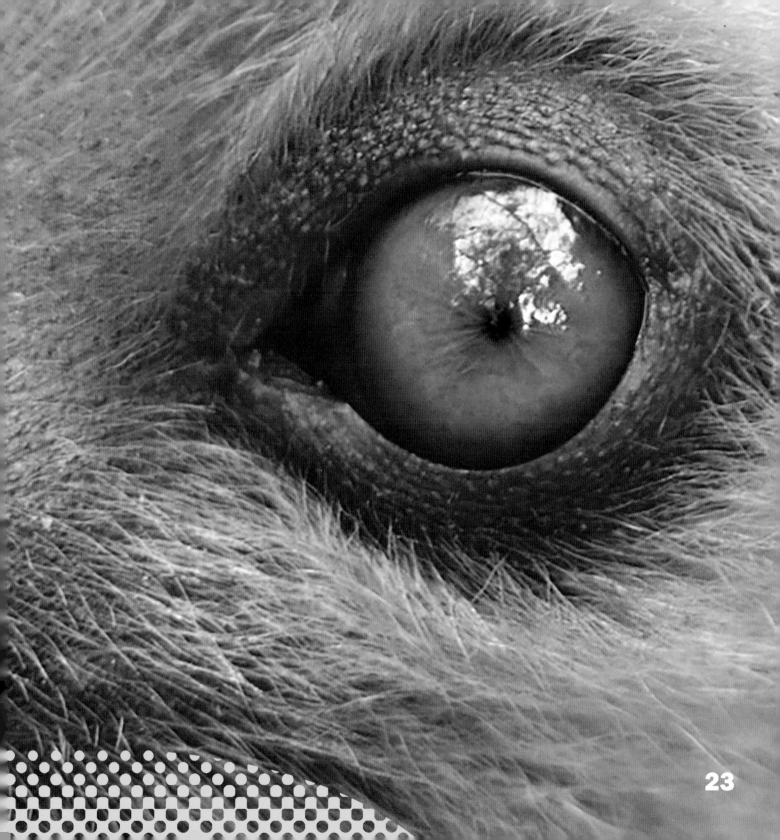

GLOSSARY

diet (DYE-uht)—the food or drink usually taken in

energy (EN-er-jee)—ability to be active

excellent (EK-suh-luhnt)—very good

munch (MUHNCH)—to eat or chew

rain forest (REYN FAWR-ist)—a tropical forest that gets a lot of rain and has tall trees

INDEX